PARANORMAL LIFE CYCLES

WEREWOLF

By
Noah Leatherland

©2024
BookLife Publishing Ltd.
King's Lynn, Norfolk
PE30 4LS, UK

All rights reserved.
Printed in India.

A catalogue record for this
book is available
from the British Library.

ISBN 978-1-80505-682-9

Written by
Noah Leatherland

Edited by
Robin Twiddy

Designed by
Jasmine Pointer

*All facts, statistics, web addresses and URLs in this book were verified as valid and accurate at time of writing.
No responsibility for any changes to external websites or references can be accepted by either the author or publisher.*

AN INTRODUCTION TO BOOKLIFE RAPID READERS...

Packed full of gripping topics and twisted tales, BookLife Rapid Readers are perfect for older children looking to propel their reading up to top speed. With three levels based on our planet's fastest animals, children will be able to find the perfect point from which to accelerate their reading journey. From the spooky to the silly, these roaring reads will turn every child at every reading level into a prolific page-turner!

CHEETAH
The fastest animals on land, cheetahs will be taking their first strides as they race to top speed.

MARLIN
The fastest animals under water, marlins will be blasting through their journey.

FALCON
The fastest animals in the air, falcons will be flying at top speed as they tear through the skies.

IMAGE CREDITS

All images courtesy of Shutterstock.com. With thanks to Getty Images, Thinkstock Photo and iStockphoto. Cover – Luca Lorenzelli, Dan Kosmayer, Sergio Photone, Here, Jakub Krechowicz, sociologas, wabeno. Recurring – Elizaveta Mironets, sociologas, wabeno. P1 – Luca Lorenzelli. 4–5 – gan chaonan, leolintang. 6–7 – e71lena, iobard. 8–9 – rudall30, MrNoe, Embrace of Beauty. 10–11 – Fernando Astasio Avila, aleks333. 12–13 – Sarah Holmlund, GSoul. 14–15 – S-BELOV, Alexander Sviridov. 16–17 – DanieleGay, Raggedstone. 18–19 – Obsidian Fantasy Studio, GSoul. 20–21 – Warm_Tail, AiiR. 22–23 – PhotoBarmaley, Hatteviden. 24–25 – Nenad.C, TeamDAF. 26–27 – VladKK, Lapa Smile. 28–29 – Julya Livshits, JM-MEDIA. 30 – Declan Hillman.

CONTENTS

PAGE 4	What Is a Life Cycle?
PAGE 6	What Is a Werewolf?
PAGE 8	The Curse Begins
PAGE 10	The Early Werewolf
PAGE 12	The Fully Transformed Werewolf
PAGE 14	Diet
PAGE 16	Habitat
PAGE 18	The Old Werewolf
PAGE 20	Passing on the Curse
PAGE 22	Types of Were-Creatures
PAGE 24	Spotting a Werewolf
PAGE 26	How to Deal with a Werewolf
PAGE 28	Life Cycle of a Werewolf
PAGE 30	Beware the Paranormal!
PAGE 31	Glossary
PAGE 32	Index

Words that look like <u>this</u> can be found in the glossary on page 31.

WHAT IS A LIFE CYCLE?

Every living thing has a life cycle. A life cycle has different steps where the living things change. The living thing might grow and look different with each new step of the cycle.

As part of the life cycle, living things will reproduce. Then, one day it is normal for them to die.

However, some things in this world are not normal. They are <u>paranormal</u>. Some things take over a normal life cycle and make it... horrific. A powerful magic can take a regular living thing and turn it into something terrifying.

This is what happens with the gory life cycle of a werewolf...

WHAT IS A WEREWOLF?

Werewolves are fierce creatures. Stories about people who turn into beasts have been told for thousands of years. Anyone that comes across a werewolf is lucky to get away alive.

The curse of the werewolf is one of the most powerful curses in the world. Once someone has been cursed, there is no way to get rid of it.

The scariest thing about a werewolf is that anyone could be one. Most of the time, they look just like a regular person. You might have already met a werewolf and not even know it.

The best way to keep yourself safe is to study them. Learn about their life cycle and you can avoid becoming a werewolf's next meal...

THE CURSE BEGINS

No one is sure how the curse of the werewolf started. Some people think it was a powerful, evil magic that turned a person into a wolf monster for the first time.

Since then, the curse has been passed on by the werewolves. All it takes is for someone to get slashed by their claws or chomped by their teeth.

Claws tearing through skin. Teeth sinking into flesh. Blood spilling from the <u>wounds</u>.

Even if the <u>victim</u> can somehow make it out of their run-in with a werewolf alive, they will be cursed. Science cannot explain it. Something about a werewolf's teeth and claws pass on the curse when they cut through skin.

THE EARLY WEREWOLF

After a bloody encounter with a werewolf, the cursed person will wake up completely fine. Once the curse takes over their body, their body heals very quickly.

To start, they will feel like they have never been healthier. But even though they feel incredible, it will not last. Everything changes when a full moon appears in the sky.

Under a full moon, their senses become much stronger, so strong that it actually starts to hurt. Noises become painfully loud. Smells become disgustingly strong. It all feels like too much.

Then, their skin starts to itch. All the hair on their body starts to get thicker and longer, ready for the next step in the life cycle.

THE FULLY TRANSFORMED WEREWOLF

At this stage of the life cycle, the cursed person begins to transform in a very painful way.

Their mouth and nose grow out into a snout, just like a wolf. Inside their mouths, their teeth get longer and sharper. They no longer look like human teeth. Instead, they look just like the deadly teeth of a wolf.

Their entire skeleton starts to change. Bones snap and then heal into completely different shapes. Their skeleton becomes something between human and wolf.

Finally, the hair on their body grows into thick, dark fur. Now, they are more like a beast than a human. They have fully transformed into a werewolf!

DIET

When someone is in their human form, they eat just like a regular person. However, when they are transformed into a werewolf, they eat like an animal.

Werewolves are excellent hunters. They are some of the deadliest <u>predators</u> in the world. It is not very often that a werewolf fails to catch its <u>prey</u>.

Werewolves are not picky eaters. They will hunt whatever they think looks like a tasty treat.

Werewolves have been known to eat all sorts of animals. The most worrying part of their diet is their taste for human flesh. Sometimes, one human is not enough to fill them up and they might eat an entire village!

HABITAT

A werewolf's habitat depends on what they are like in their human form. Many cursed people live near forests so that when they transform, they can hide in the woodland.

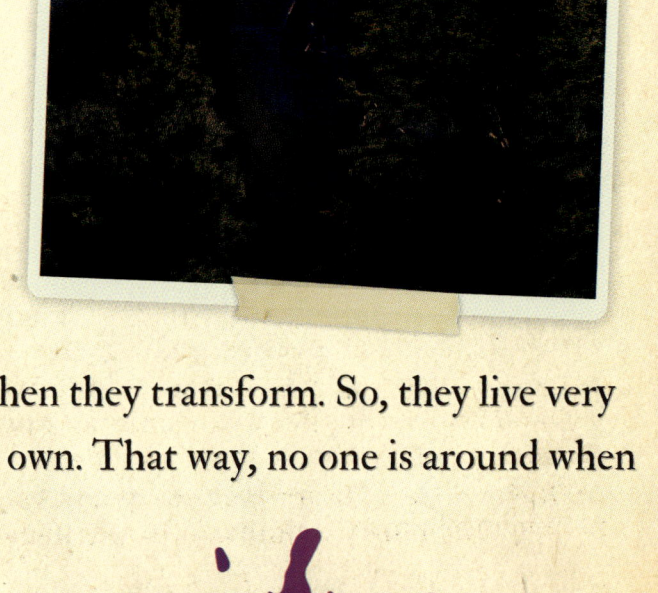

Some cursed people are very worried about hurting others when they transform. So, they live very far away on their own. That way, no one is around when they transform.

Others might try to blend in as their human form. They might live in cities, towns and villages with normal humans. There are some things they can do to make things less dangerous when they transform.

When they feel the curse changing them, they might lock themselves in a basement or chain themselves up.

THE
OLD WEREWOLF

The longer someone carries the werewolf's curse, the stronger it becomes. As the curse becomes more powerful, their transformations become even more horrifying.

Older werewolves are much bigger. Their teeth and claws become longer, sharper and more deadly.

Like other animals, as a werewolf gets older, their fur starts to turn grey. Some say they have seen completely silver werewolves.

A full moon <u>triggers</u> a werewolf's transformation. As werewolves get older, some of them can get better at controlling the transformation.

However, some of them lose all control of the curse. There are some werewolves that cannot change back into a human. They are stuck being a giant beast for the rest of their lives.

PASSING ON
THE CURSE

Although regular wolves hunt in packs, werewolves usually hunt by themselves. They are very <u>aggressive</u> towards other werewolves and do not like to share their food.

Werewolves track down their prey with their strong sense of smell. They might hide at first, but once they have their target in sight, they pounce.

Werewolves do not think about passing on the curse when they hunt. That is why werewolves are so rare. They tend to eat every bit of their prey.

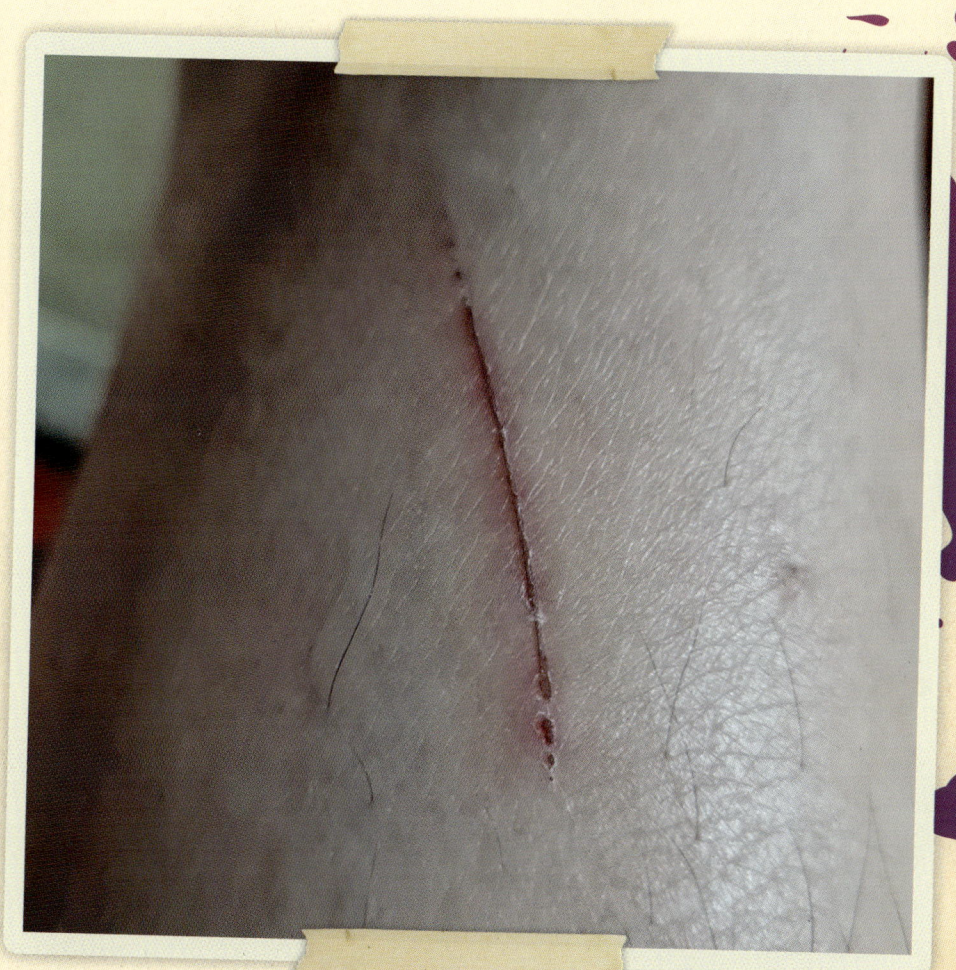

The curse will pass on to the few who can escape a werewolf with just a wound. Even the smallest scratch can pass on the curse.

TYPES OF WERE-CREATURES

Other magical curses can turn people into other types of were-beasts. The full moon can make all of them transform into their beastly forms.

WEREBEAR

Werebears are very similar to werewolves. Someone cursed to become a werebear transforms into a frightening grizzly bear when the Moon is full.

WERERABBIT

Sometimes, people are cursed to transform into huge, terrifying versions of smaller animals. When someone is cursed to be a wererabbit, the full moon transforms them into a giant rabbit monster.

Just like the werewolf, it only takes a bite or a scratch from one of these creatures to pass their curse on.

SPOTTING A WEREWOLF

People with the werewolf's curse look like regular people most of the time. However, there are some things to look out for.

ACTING LIKE A DOG

Sometimes, people can still feel like a wolf in their human form. They might chew on something like it is a bone. They might be strangely interested in certain smells.

FULL MOON

People carrying the werewolf's curse can get very restless around a full moon. Watch how someone acts when there is a full moon out at night.

Do they hide away from the moonlight and tuck themselves away? Or do they disappear... and you soon hear a wolf's howl in the distance?

HOW TO DEAL WITH A WEREWOLF

There are a few things you can do to keep werewolves away.

SILVER

There are not many things that can hurt a werewolf, but silver is believed to be one of them. Silver burns werewolves. Even something as small as a silver coin can hurt.

Keep plenty of silver things around to stop werewolves getting too close.

FLOWERS

Werewolves have a very good sense of smell. Sometimes, strong smells can become too much for them. Some stories say that flowers are a good way to stop werewolves from getting too close.

Growing strong smelling flowers around your home might just keep you safe from any werewolves nearby.

You can ask a werewolf hunter to help keep you safe!

Life Cycle of a
WEREWOLF

The life cycle of a werewolf starts with the curse. Just a scratch or a bite from a werewolf is enough to pass the curse onto the next person.

Once they become cursed, the person will start to feel incredible... until the full moon comes out. Then, the curse takes over and the transformation begins!

Their mouth and nose stretch out into a wolf's snout. Dark fur grows all over their body. Their skeletons shift and change, turning them into a fearsome monster. They have become a werewolf!

They scurry off into the night looking for their next meal. If they come across an unlucky person, they might pass the curse on... as long as they do not eat them whole...

BEWARE THE PARANORMAL!

The world has lots of weird and bizarre paranormal creatures hidden in the shadows. However, you should be careful. They can be very dangerous and you should never go looking for them.

The best way to stay safe and explore the paranormal world is to read and learn all about these creepy creatures.

GLOSSARY

AGGRESSIVE   likely to attack

PREDATORS   animals that hunt other animals for food

PREY   animals that are hunted by other animals for food

REPRODUCE   to make more of the same thing

PARANORMAL   something that cannot be explained by science

TRANSFORM   to turn into something else

TRIGGERS   causes something to happen

VICTIM   someone who has something bad done to them

WOUNDS   injuries such as cuts and scratches

INDEX

CLAWS 8–9, 18

FLOWERS 27

FUR 13, 18, 29

MOON 10–11, 19, 22–23, 25, 28

PREY 14, 20–21

SILVER 18, 26

TEETH 8–9, 12, 18

VILLAGES 15, 17

WOUNDS 9, 21